This book belongs to

....

....

PAW PATROL™: 2019

A CENTUM BOOK 978-1-912707-18-8

Published in Great Britain by Centum Books Ltd

This edition published 2018

1 3 5 7 9 10 8 6 4 2

Centum Books Ltd, 20 Devon Square, Newton Abbot, Devon, TQ12 2HR, UK

books@centumbooksltd.co.uk

CENTUM BOOKS Limited Reg. No. 07641486

A CIP catalogue record for this book is available from the British Library

Printed in Italy

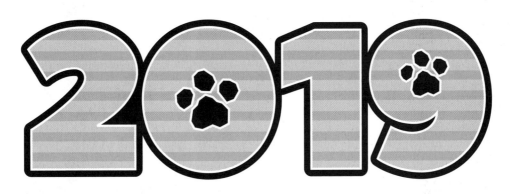

centum

Contents

Welcome to Adventure Bay

Whenever there is trouble in Adventure Bay, the PAW Patrol is always ready to race to the rescue. The pups are raring to go, go, go!

Ryder

Rocky

Tracker

Chase

Skye

Marshall

Zuma

Rubble

Everest

Chase

Chase is a top police dog. His Pup Pack opens to give him a megaphone, a searchlight, and a net that shoots out to catch things.

Net shoots out here

Pup Pack

Name: Chase
Breed: German Shepherd
Skills: Herding traffic, blocking off dangerous roads and solving mysteries.

Did you know?
Chase can sniff out anything, but he happens to be allergic to both cats and feathers!

Megaphone

My nose knows!

Chase needs to get to the Lookout. Help guide him through the streets of Adventure Bay, avoiding the kittens.

START →

Can you spot the pup treat?

Colour in Chase's badge when you find it.

FINISH →

Answers on page 60.

9

Pup, pup and away

Prepare for take-off with the Air Patrol. Find your brightest pencils or crayons, then colour in the pups. Don't forget their PAWsome Air Patroller!

Can you spot the pup treat?

Colour in Chase's badge when you find it.

To the Lookout

The pups have lost some of their favourite things. Can you spot all of the items in the big picture? Tick each one when you find it.

Can you spot the pup treat?

Colour in Chase's badge when you find it.

Which pup is missing?

.... is missing

Answers on page 60.

13

Get to know the pups

Marshall

Marshall is a brave fire dog. His Pup Pack contains an amazing fire hose with two water jets.

Double-spray fire hose

Pup Pack

Name: Marshall
Breed: Dalmatian
Skills: Can smell and detect gas leaks and smoke, and is really fast at running.

Did you know?
He gets too excited and can be a little clumsy!

Ready for a ruff, ruff rescue

Design an obstacle course so Marshall can practise his fire-rescue skills.

Why not add some rubble for Marshall to get past?

Did someone say 'Rubble'?

Add some cones for Marshall to go around.

Can you spot the pup treat?

Colour in Marshall's badge when you find it.

You could draw some wooden obstacles for Marshall to jump over.

Playful colouring

It's PAWfectly simple!

You can use this picture as a guide.

Dot-to-spot

Marshall is an amazing fire-rescue pup.
Join the dots to complete the picture,
then colour in the PAWsome rescue pup!

I'm **fired up!**

Can you spot the pup treat?

Colour in Marshall's badge when you find it.

Answers on page 60.

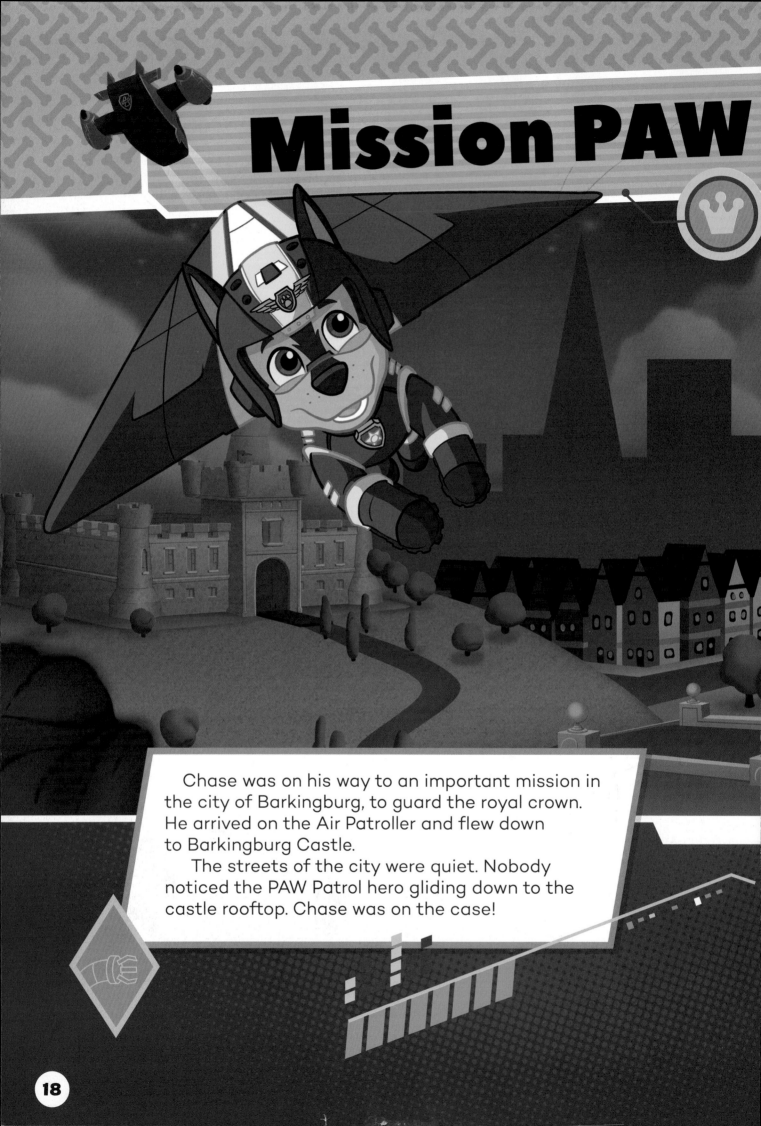

Mission PAW

Chase was on his way to an important mission in the city of Barkingburg, to guard the royal crown. He arrived on the Air Patroller and flew down to Barkingburg Castle.

The streets of the city were quiet. Nobody noticed the PAW Patrol hero gliding down to the castle rooftop. Chase was on the case!

Chase quickly changed into his smartest outfit, with a special Pup Tag bow tie. Then he met the Princess of Barkingburg, her uncle the Earl and her pup Sweetie. "I'm so glad you could help us," said the Princess.

"I like your bow tie," said Sweetie and smiled at Chase. "Thanks," said Chase. "It helps me stay in contact with Ryder." He didn't mention the camera hidden inside it. That was his superspy secret!

That night, Chase stood on guard by the crown. It had a powerful alarm beam switched on around it. Everything seemed safe....

Suddenly, Chase began to sneeze. Someone had let kittens into the room, and he was allergic to them!

A huge sneeze sent Chase tumbling backwards into the alarm beam. The alarm wailed loudly. He had to find a way to turn it off, and do it fast.

At last Chase managed it. But when he turned back the crown was gone!

Chase used his great sense of smell to follow the thief's trail, but as he turned a corner in the Castle he was shocked to see Sweetie trying on the crown.

"That kitten trick worked brilliantly. Now look at me. I would make the perfect queen," she giggled, as she admired her reflection.

Sweetie caught a glimpse of Chase as he called Ryder on his bow tie Pup Tag.

"No you don't," she growled. She grabbed the bow tie and pressed a button that opened a trapdoor, sending Chase plunging down into a dungeon.

Chase was trapped! Meanwhile Sweetie ran to the Princess and told her that Chase had stolen the royal crown.

"I will have to tell Ryder straight away. One of his pups has gone bad," the Earl sighed, shaking his head.

When Ryder got the call, he didn't believe for one moment that Chase was guilty.

"Chase needs help," he said. "Come on PAW Patrol. It's Mission PAW time!"

The Air Patroller got the PAW Patrol to Barkingburg fast, and they were soon ready for action using their all-new Mission PAW equipment.

Sweetie had thrown the bow tie into the castle moat. Zuma dived into the water in his Aqua Drone, using sonar to locate the bow tie's signal.

Chase heard his friend through the wall of his dungeon and used his tennis ball cannon to fire balls at the wall.

Bang! Bang!

"What's that?" cried Zuma, hearing the thuds through his sonar. The banging noise helped Ryder and the pups locate Chase in the dungeon.

Now it was Rubble's turn to help.

"Rubble on the double!" he called and turned on his amazing Mini Miner. *Whirrrrrrrr.*

The Mini Miner was perfect for breaking through the wall of the castle to get to Chase's dungeon.

"Am I glad to see you!" cried Chase. He quickly told his friends what Sweetie had done. "My bow tie camera filmed everything," he explained.

Ryder showed the bow tie film to the Princess and the Earl, proving once and for all who the thief really was. But Sweetie had already escaped, taking the crown with her.

Sweetie had her own flying vehicle but she had met her match in Skye, who put her Sky Cycle into helicopter mode and chased her down. Sweetie was caught PAW Patrol style!

"I'm sorry for thinking you were the thief, Chase," said the Princess. "You are a very brave pup, and so are your friends."

"If you ever need us again, just yelp for help," Ryder told the grateful Princess. "No job is too big, no pup is too small!"

Recall to action

The PAW Patrol has just completed another successful mission in Adventure Bay. Look at this picture for 30 seconds. Then cover the bottom half of these pages with paper and try to answer the questions. If you like, you can write your answers on the paper.

Can you spot the pup treat?

Colour in Chase's badge when you find it.

1. Which pup is licking Ryder's cheek?

2. Are Skye's goggles blue or pink?

3. Which pup is wearing a red Pup Pack?

4. What is Zuma carrying in his mouth?

5. Is Everest next to Marshall or next to Skye?

6. Is Rubble wearing his yellow helmet?

Answers on page 60.

Rubble

Rubble is a tough construction dog. His Pup Pack opens to reveal a bucket arm scoop for digging and lifting large and heavy objects.

Name: Rubble
Breed: Bulldog
Skills: Superior digging and construction skills, plus he's an excellent skate and snow boarder.

Did you know?
He doesn't like spiders or being in deep water.

Bucket scoop

28

Rubble on the double

Rubble loves to dig. Can you spot the picture of this ruff, tough pup below that is different from the rest?

a

b

Can you spot the pup treat?

Colour in Chase's badge when you find it.

c

d

Answers on page 60.

Pup patterns

Complete the patterns by working out which picture comes next in each row. Use the key below and write the letter of the correct picture in each empty shield.

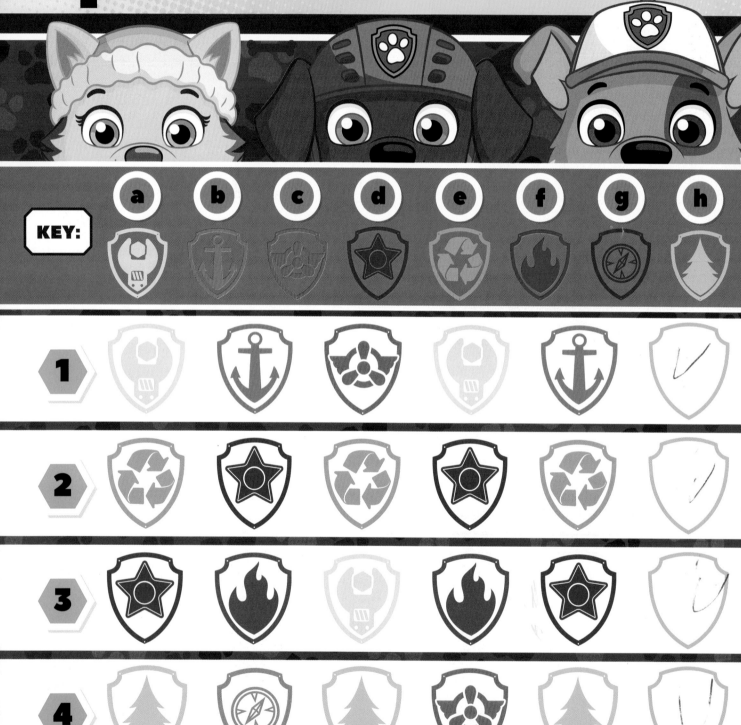

KEY:

a b c d e f g h

1

2

3

4

Can you spot the pup treat?

Colour in Chase's badge when you find it.

Time for treats

Help Marshall find the bowl of tasty treats. He can only step on the paw prints in the order shown below. He can move forwards, backwards up and down.

FOLLOW THIS ORDER

START

FINISH

Can you spot the pup treat?

Colour in Chase's badge when you find it.

Answers on page 60.

Counting on you

If you're in trouble, you can rely on the PAW Patrol to help out!
Look at this page, then use your number skills to count up the pup pictures.

Can you spot the pup treat?

Colour in Chase's badge when you find it.

1 Marshall
Circle the right number:
1 2 3 4 5 6 7 8 9 10

2 Skye
Circle the right number:
1 2 3 4 5 6 7 8 9 10

3 Zuma
Circle the right number:
1 2 3 4 5 6 7 8 9 10

4 Rocky
Circle the right number:
1 2 3 4 5 6 7 8 9 10

Home sweet home

Ryder and the PAW Patrol love their Lookout in Adventure Bay! Draw lines to link the missing pieces to the correct place in the picture.

Can you spot the pup treat?

Colour in Skye's badge when you find it.

Answers on page 61.

33

Get to know the pups

Skye

Skye is a pilot dog. Her Pup Pack opens to reveal wings that allow her to fly.

Flying goggles

Wings

Pup Pack

Name: Skye
Breed: Cockapoo
Skills: High-flying rescues!
She is a fearless daredevil who
will try anything with a smile.

Did you know?
Skye loves playing her favourite
video game, *Pup Pup Boogie*.

This pup's gotta fly!

Skye has been busy flying over Adventure Bay and taking pictures. Draw a line to match up each photograph with the correct location.

c. Seal Island

d. Farmer Yumi's Farm

a. The Pup Park

e. The train station

b. The PAW Patrol Lookout

The PAW Patrol is on the job!

The PAW Patrol is lined up and ready for action! As soon as a call comes in, it's all paws on deck. Take a look at the pup pictures, then answer the questions.

Who is the tallest member of the team?

Who is the smallest member of the team?

Which pups are wearing green hats?

Which pups are wearing helmets?

Which pup has got a woolly hat on?

CDECNR

Which pup is wearing a police hat?

Can you spot the pup treat?

Colour in Skye's badge when you find it.

Answers on page 61.

37

It's a jungle out there!

Get ready to go jungle tracking with the PAW Patrol. Each picture in the panel along the bottom appears somewhere in the big picture. Can you find them all?

Can you spot the pup treat?

Colour in Tracker's badge when you find it.

Can you spot these, too?

Rocky

Rocky is a creative recycling pup. His Pup Pack contains a mechanical claw, as well as tools like a screwdriver and ratchet.

Mechanical claw

Tools in pack

Screwdriver

Name: Rocky
Breed: Mixed breed
Skills: Reducing, reusing and recycling anything he can find.

Did you know?
Rocky is not a fan of baths and doesn't like getting wet at all.

Ready, steady, Rocky!

Help Rocky complete these picture patterns. Point to the object that comes next in each row, and then write the correct letter in the circle.

 1

 2

 3

Can you spot the pup treat?

Colour in Rocky's badge when you find it.

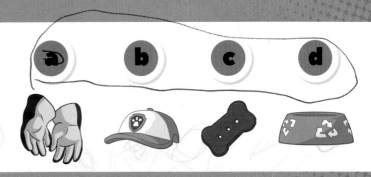

Colouring code:
TEAMWORK

The PAW Patrol has its very own superpower, TEAMWORK!
Colour the picture using the colour key below.
There is a guide at the top of the opposite
page to help you.

Wow!

1 2   2 1   3   4

42

Yelp for help!

Uh oh! The name of each pup has been mixed up. Write the correct name below the jumbled up version, then draw a line to the correct pup on the opposite page.

1

CSAHE

2

MRAASHLL

3

RCKOY

4

YKSE

5

ZMAU

6

RBULBE

7

RACTKER

8

RESTEVE

44

Can you spot the pup treat?

Colour in Zuma's badge when you find it.

Zuma

Zuma is the team's water rescue dog. His Pup Pack contains air tanks and propellers so he can dive and swim deep underwater.

Name: Zuma
Breed: Labrador
Skills: Excellent at swimming and diving.

Did you know?
Zuma has lots of energy for any adventure in store for him!

Air tanks

46

Let's dive in!

Can you spot the pup treat?

Colour in Zuma's badge when you find it.

It's time for an underwater adventure! Can you help Zuma count the fish?

1 How many can you count?

2 How many can you count?

3 How many can you count?

Get to know the pups

Tracker

Tracker is the team's jungle rescue dog. His Pup Pack has a multitool, cables and a grappling hook that he often uses to swing on branches.

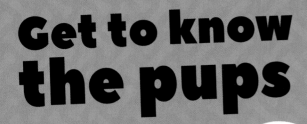

Name: Tracker
Breed: Potcake
Skills: Strong sense of hearing and can pick up on tiny sounds. He can also speak Spanish.

Did you know?
Tracker is brave but he doesn't like being in dark places.

Multitool

Cables

Jungle rescue

Uh oh! Rubble, Chase and Marshall are lost in the jungle. Help Tracker follow the right path to find his pup pals.

START →

Can you spot the pup treat?

Colour in Tracker's badge when you find it.

FINISH →

Answers on page 61.

51

Meet Tracker

The PAW Patrol's friend Carlos was busy digging for treasure in the jungle.

"I love discovering new things," he said to himself as he worked. "The jungle is a beautiful place, too. I must tell Ryder what a great spot this is."

Ryder was excited to hear about the dig.

"Hey, Carlos! Do you need any help?" he asked over the PupPad.

"No, I'm fine. I'm having a great time," said Carlos. "I'll call you as soon as I find treasure!"

"Okay," laughed Ryder. "We'll be ready to roll when you need us."

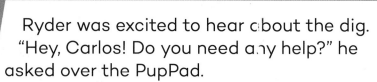

As Carlos was chatting he stepped forwards.

"Waaah!" he cried.

He had tumbled into a deep hole, and it was too steep for him to climb out! He had dropped his phone, too, but luckily Ryder had seen everything on his PupPad.

"PAW Patrol, to the PAW Patroller!" Ryder cried. "We've got to rumble to the jungle to save Carlos."

The pups raced aboard their rescue vehicles. But how were they going to find the hole in the jungle and rescue their friend?

Meanwhile, Carlos was trapped and he couldn't reach his phone. "Help! I'm down here," he shouted.

Luckily for Carlos and the PAW Patrol, there was a very special dog in the jungle that day. The pup had big ears that helped him to hear noises from far away. He picked up the sound of Carlos shouting and raced towards him.

The jungle pup soon found the hole. "My name is Tracker and I'll do whatever it takes to rescue you," he called to Carlos.

"I'm trapped! Can you find my phone and give my friends directions to this hole?" asked Carlos.

"Sí! I'm on it," said Tracker.

Tracker quickly found Carlos's phone. He pressed the screen and it rang through to the PAW Patroller. The pup crew were surprised to see a dog they'd never met before.

"Buenos días. My name is Tracker," he said. "I'll help guide you to the hole where your amigo is trapped."

"Thanks, Tracker. Good to meet you," replied Ryder. "We're on our way."

SsSsSsSsS ...

As Tracker was speaking to the PAW Patrol, a dangerous snake was slithering towards the hole. It was the longest, hungriest, meanest snake in the jungle....

"Hey, Señor Slithery. Back off!" Tracker called as he leaped in front of the scary snake.

Down below in the hole, Carlos could hear Tracker barking.

"That's one brave pup," he said.

The snake wasn't scared away for long, but the PAW Patrol arrived just in time to help. They used the PAW Patroller horn to blast out noise that made the reptile slither off for good.

"The PAW Patrol is on a roll!" cried Ryder as they raced towards the hole.

Chase used his night-vision goggles to spot their friend at the bottom of the hole. Then he guided the winch from the back of his vehicle down to Carlos.

"Winch! Retract!" Chase barked, and the winch pulled Carlos up safely.

Finally, Marshall used his X-ray equipment to check that Carlos wasn't hurt.

"I'm fine," he confirmed.

"For being such a brave pup and saving Carlos, we'd like you to join the PAW Patrol, Tracker," said Ryder.

Tracker was given his very own Pup Pack and Pup Tag, with a picture of a tracking compass on it.

"I can't wait to see how this all works," he grinned.

"You look awesome," said Marshall.

Rocky showed Tracker how to use the new Pup Pack before he tried it out.

"Multitool," barked Tracker. Instantly, a robot tool arm slid out from the pack. It had lots of great tools on the end for different jobs.

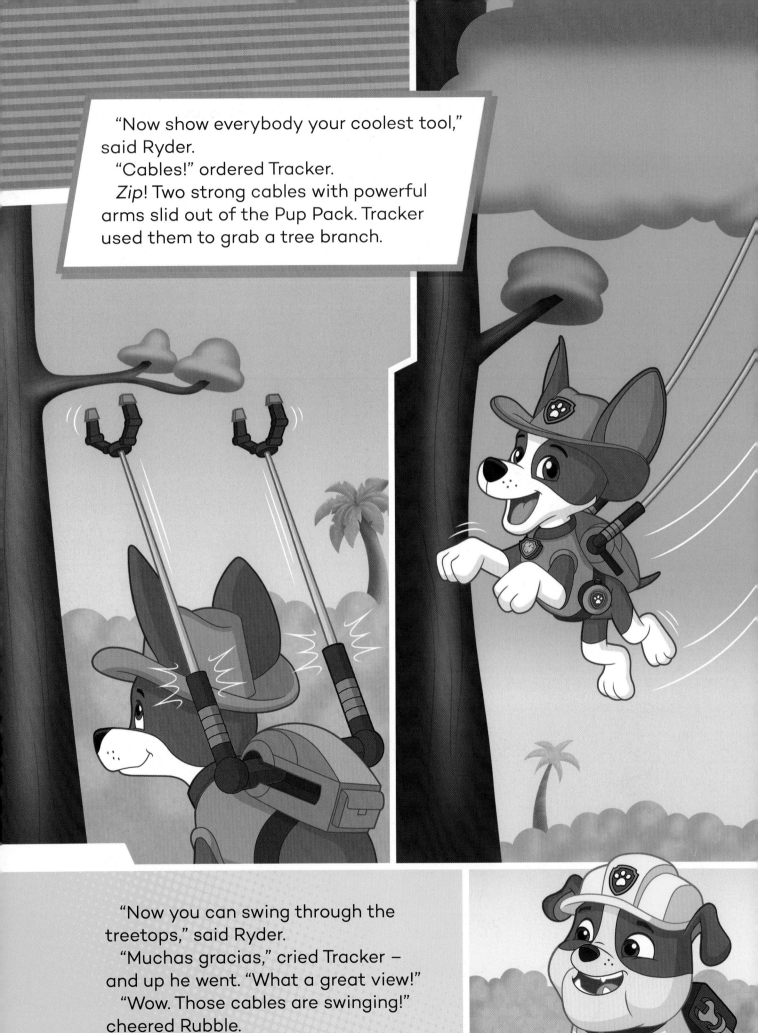

"Now show everybody your coolest tool," said Ryder.

"Cables!" ordered Tracker.

Zip! Two strong cables with powerful arms slid out of the Pup Pack. Tracker used them to grab a tree branch.

"Now you can swing through the treetops," said Ryder.

"Muchas gracias," cried Tracker – and up he went. "What a great view!"

"Wow. Those cables are swinging!" cheered Rubble.

"Muchas gracias," said Tracker,
"I'm all ears and now I'm all gears, too."
"Welcome to the PAW Patrol,"
said Ryder.
"Get ready to rumble in the
jungle with us any time!"

There was one more
gift for Tracker as
a reward for his bravery.
It was a super-cool
jeep, just right for
jungle adventures.
    "A jeep? Just for me?"
asked Tracker.
    "Sí!" cried the pup crew.

Answers

Page 9

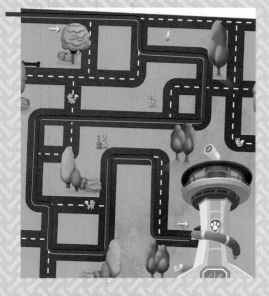

Pages 12-13

Zuma is missing

Page 17

Pages 26-27

1. Chase
2. Pink
3. Marshall
4. Bone
5. Marshall
6. No

Page 29

Rubble C is the different Rubble

Page 30

Page 31

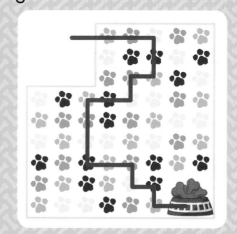

Page 32

1. 5 Marshalls
2. 3 Skyes
3. 5 Zumas
4. 7 Rockys

Page 33
1b, 2d, 3a, 4c

Page 35
1c, 2b, 3e, 4a, 5d

Pages 36-37
Chase is the tallest member
of the team
Skye is the smallest member
of the team
Rocky and Tracker are wearing
green hats
Marshall, Zuma and Rubble are
wearing helmets
Everest has got a woolly hat on
Chase is wearing a police hat

Pages 38-39

Page 41
1c, 2d, 3b

Pages 42-43
15 stars

Pages 44-45
1. CHASE, 2. MARSHALL, 3. ROCKY
4. SKYE, 5. ZUMA, 6. RUBBLE
7. TRACKER, 8. EVEREST

Page 47
1. 3
2. 3
3. 2

Page 51